Writings About My World

Madeline Sharples

Copyright© 2025 Madeline Sharples
ISBN: 978-93-6354-500-7

First Edition: 2025
Rs. 200/-

Cyberwit.net
HIG 45 Kaushambi Kunj, Kalindipuram
Allahabad - 211011 (U.P.) India
http://www.cyberwit.net
Tel: +(91) 9415091004
E-mail: info@cyberwit.net

Printed at Repro India Limited.

Contents

OBSERVATIONS

Gunning It

The woman in the back seat
kept the pressure on:
Turn here, turn there
No, you're in the wrong lane
Get over to the right,
No, the left
We'll never make it on time
You have to gun it
Gun it, the pedal to the metal
until we could stand it
no longer.

There is no gunning
a Toyota Prius
It's too much of a gentle car
It's driver a steady, thoughtful guy,
not used to such backseat tirades.
And you know what?
pretty soon
we were there
only six minutes late
And we didn't need
no stinkin' gunning at all.

What's Junk About That?

Can you imagine recent studies
say obesity in children
is not related to their
consumption of junk food
in the schools?
Can you imagine
they say children form
their eating habits at home,
so why worry about limiting
their junk food consumption
outside the home?
Can you imagine why?
Of course, you guessed it.
The schools get a profit –
probably a huge profit
from those ubiquitous vending machines
that spit forth,
with the drop of a few coins,
a constant supply of
high-sugar soft drinks, chocolate bars,
chocolate chip cookies, and chips.
You name it, if it's junk, it's there.

The food hustlers entice school management
to allow them to put the machines on their sites
in exchange for bonuses.
The food hustlers are only
about selling and money.

The food hustlers could care less
about healthy children.

And then on top of all that
these poor children eat
burgers dripping with cheese
or pizza practically every night
for dinner at home.
So the problem is not only in the schools.
Their mothers are too busy
or too uninformed
to make them a proper meal.

How astonishing that parents and teachers
allow this behavior.
The children eat and binge
binge and eat.
until they become
a generation that will not survive
long enough to become viable adults.
They will be too sick with heart problems
and diabetes to work and have a family,

Suffice it to say,
we need to take the plunge
and get that junk stuff out of the school
and off our pantry shelves.
Neither our families nor our nation
can afford to do anything less.

Magic Potion

I see deep furrows in my face
over my eyes, across my forehead,
from my nostrils, down into my chin.
They look like scars, my niece says
like her daddy has around his mouth.
Mine are the scars of age
earned through years of child rearing
work, parent care,
sleepless nights and my son's death.
But, I'll not let them be.
My needle-wielding dermatologist
injects each line with a magic potion
that will give me an illusion of youth
for another few months or so.

Always Tired

This morning I'm wide awake
after a long sleep – at least for me –
over six hours.
I'm running myself ragged
Up every morning before dawn
to go to the gym
driving the freeways all over LA
to get to work
doing the shopping, the cooking, the laundry
making sure every crease is smoothed out
when I make the bed before I leave home
and plucking every stray eyebrow
out of my forehead
before I go to bed at night.
I even have the words, WRITE, WRITE, WRITE,
in capital letters on my mobile phone.
If I don't check the box off everyday
I feel guilty.
So, last night I gave myself permission to relax
to feel blissful
to breathe in the pine and sulfur and salt air
to leisurely walk in the garden
and look at the lily pads.
My body won't fall apart if I miss a day's work out,
but, if I don't stop pushing myself,
someday I won't wake up.

The Failed Nest

The little dove's
peaceful demeanor
belies her failed nest.
Her tiny head, not quite fitting
her gray and plump physique,
stays straight ahead
in denial
that all her attempts
did not produce a place
for her expectant brood
to bloom and grow.

From my sink I watched her
gather twig after twig
and lay each one carefully
on the top of my kitchen greenhouse window.
Some fell to the ground immediately
from the slanted glass
while others remain to remind her and me
of how she botched her job.

And as she sits,
perhaps looking for a tree limb,
a building ledge,
or a small patch of vegetation
on which to rebuild,
her coo-OO-ooing lamentations
just make me want to cry.

I go out to see
what I can do to help,
but she suddenly ascends.
Her long, slender tail streams out
to form a perfect vee with her
stretched-out wings.
I guess she just can't face me
and admit her defeat.

White Parasol

I saw her round the corner,
a young woman with long black plated hair.
So pretty, she didn't need make up,
wearing a longish full-skirted dress
in a color I can't describe.
Maybe mint or olive
and a sparkling necklace
of crystal-like beads around her neck.
But what got my attention was
the little white parasol she carried with ruffles
around the edge and a long,
pronounced ferrule at the top.
It wasn't common here on
Greenwich Village streets,
so I wondered about her.
Where she came from, what she was doing here.
The air was thick and humid, and I was sweating
so much I had to keep mopping my brow
with my already saturated handkerchief,
envying the woman under that dainty canopy.
It must have kept her cool.
I decided to duck into place up the street – the Red Palace,
a dive I've been going to
for well over twenty years.
They served a passable chicken dim sum
and homemade green tea ice cream
that made my tongue sizzle.
I'd wait out the heat there even if it took all night.
But I kept thinking about the woman with the parasol,

and wish she were sitting across from me
and talking to me about her life.
I imagined she came from some exotic Asian city,
Maybe Singapore – A place I've longed to go for so long
I can't even say.
When I looked it up last year, they said,
Singapore is ranked at or near the top in mathematical ability
and boasts one of the most admired education systems in the
world.
I bet the lady with that plush white parasol doesn't know that.
But one thing I know for sure.
If she were my daughter,
I'd send her to a convent
rather than let her out alone.
She wouldn't be traveling these crowded streets
if I had anything to say about it.
And then I looked in the mirror above me
and saw her entering my little restaurant –
certainly not good enough for this beauty.
I spun around to face her and smiled.
But she ignored me. Really what did I expect?
I'm an old man who could be her father.
What would she do with someone like me?
Instead the waiter escorted her to the corner table,
lit the candle and handed her a menu,
as she sat down.
Again, I wondered, could she have come from someplace
like Stockholm where they wore furs
instead of parasols, where the archipelago –
a cluster of some 30,000 islands,
islets, and rocks twenty minutes
away from Stockholm city – is one of the most
spectacular sites I've ever seen.

I finally decided to be on my way
and get realistic about what would be next in my life.
I'd done enough fantasizing
about things that could never be.
Maybe I'd get out away from the crowds
and noise of this city
and go up to the mountains and raise bees.
I'd probably never see a pretty girl with a white
parasol there.

Invisible

They look through me
the brawny young guys
flexing their biceps
as they reach for the shoulder press.
Eyes fixed on the girl
in sleek black tights
boobs bursting out of her bra
strong and slim and self-confident
strutting past
tilting her head back
to take a swig of water

They look past me
the sweaty runners
in tank tops and Adidas shorts
and hairy calf muscles
forming a perfect Vee.
They see the far away figure
gliding on roller blades
flowing blonde hair
showing more tan than thong.
Fit and firm
she moves closer
smiles wide
and raises her hand
to give them a high five.

Look at me
I'm firm and slim.

Underneath my baggy tee and sweats
I feel only 28
though my hair is almost white
and my face has lines impossible to erase.
In a world of fleeting youth
blind to the reality of old age
give me a glance
a glimmer of recognition
that I still exist

I Just Love My Boss

I have nothing but respect for the man I work for.
He can waltz into work like the 10:00 scholar
without feeling one iota of guilt.
And that he's gotten away with working part time
for full-time pay for the last 20 years
is something I want to strive for.
Just looking at him shows how cool and with it he is.
He has a bald head
slightly flat in the back rimmed by a fringe
of white hair that just graces his shoulders.
He always wears black or gray dress shirts
sleeves neatly folded
and open at the collar to show off his bare chest.
That his shirts show a hint of wet circles under his arms
means he's been having a particularly hard and productive day.
He always wears suspenders to hold up his loose-fitting trousers.
with hems almost reaching his ankles.

When he comes into my office I almost go into a swoon.
He pulls his chair up close to mine
so I can inhale his strong, masculine aroma.
I can also watch how he blows and carefully wipes his nose
into a freshly ironed and neatly folded white handkerchief.
Afterward he folds the cloth right up
and puts it back into his pocket.

But, alas, he comes to see me only for business.
His directions totally engage me.

Bear with me, he says over and over to get his points across.
When he finishes I'm hooked.
This is a man, who knows how to motivate,
and I'm always ready to follow his lead.

The Couple at the Gym

He reminds me of a Svengali as he waits for her at the bench.
In his baseball hat and long sweats,
his backpack slung over one shoulder,
he paces, looks around, adjusts his workout gloves
until she appears.
Her black hair is done up in a ponytail, she has a movie star's
face,
and a body without a pinch of fat.
He leads, she follows him into the gym
and they workout side by side
on equipment he chooses.
He hands her the weights,
she complies with the dictated reps.
He finds two treadmills for their next set
and she like the good girl
jumps on one of them and performs.
They don't talk except when he orders her to pick up her speed.
He's too occupied singing along with the music
flowing through his ear buds.
She just works out, looking pretty.
And so it goes.
Svengali and the good girl.
I see them everyday at the gym.

Writer's Block

It's not usual for me
to sit and look
at the blank page
and have nothing come.
So, I'll write about nothing coming
from this poet's brain this afternoon.
Even as I write I need to stop
and think and go back and edit,
something I almost never do.
I usually write, keeping my fingers moving
on the keyboard until I finish.
And then I go back and read
and edit and maybe do a little rewrite.
But, this is not a usual writing day.
I am stumped.
I can't think of anyone I don't know
to write about.
My poem a week challenge to myself
may have to remain unfulfilled today.
Instead I write about this unknown
thing about myself and pretty soon
the page once blank seems
to be filling up with words
and I'll come to the end of it
and perhaps forgivingly let myself
and my challenge off the hook
and call it a day.

Recognized from Behind

I walked behind her
and instantly knew
her gait, her short stringy blond hair
the way she held her arms.
And though I didn't immediately
recall her name
I knew who she was.
We hadn't spoken in years
maybe once at the coffee shop.
She gave me a hug
not like her at all.
Like when I knew her
on our tennis team.
she wouldn't let me play
not because I wasn't good enough
just because she had the power
not to.
So, did I rush up to her and say hello
glad to see you.
Are you a new member of the gym?
You bet I didn't
I could go another many years
without her back in my life.

I Saw Myself the Other Day

I stopped for a cup of tea
at the Galleria food court.
To my left sat a mother
with her two little ones.
She spoon fed a baby boy
from a thermos.
An older girl ate by herself
from a box of McDonalds'
chicken fingers.
I watched the girl eat
dipping one finger at a time
in sauce, and then go back for more.
Sometimes she got up,
peeked in the stroller
picked up a toy
and then sat down again
and ate some more.
This girl was well on her way
to being as round as her mother.
Her thick thighs
chubby arms
and protruding belly
showed those fried chicken fingers
weren't the best food choice
for her to eat.
And she could have been pretty
with her long wavy dark brown hair
just how I looked at that age
just how I ate too.

My father and brother called me fatty
something I never forgot
when I would dig in to eat.
Perhaps this little girl needs some ridicule too
though a thinner and more attentive mother
would help even more.

A New Friend

We met by phone.
I have no idea what she looks like.
And within minutes I could tell
we are in for a long, long friendship.
She too lost a son to suicide.
And after a year and a half she
cannot find an inch of space
to get out of her grief.
She thinks she should be better by now.
I told her there are no shoulds
in this grieving game.
And while crying she told me
how guilty she feels
even though there was nothing
she could have done to stop it.
And we went back and forth like that
for a while.
This new friendship will be good
for both of us although I'll try
to listen more than tell.

My Family Heirloom

The pitcher stands tall on the
bookcase in our bedroom
like a posed flamingo
with painted deco geometrics
in deep magentas and greens
trimmed in gold leaf.
I don't know its history except
it came to our family from Europe
sometime in the 1920s.
I remember seeing it
first at my grandmother's
atop her armoire in her tiny
seventh floor walk-up apartment
on Chicago's West Side.
When she died it came to my parent's
where it always stood
on a mantel in Chicago, Los Angeles,
Culver City or wherever else they lived
until my mother gave it to me.
I never told her how much I wanted it.
Somehow, she just knew.

Thirteen Months

Every morning I swiped my badge into the reader
to gain access into my work facility.
I walked down the long corridor to the office
I shared with John.
It had two desks, a table, a tall filing cabinet
a white board with closing doors and
the requisite desk chairs, guests chairs, telephones, and computers.
That's all.
The walls were bare. Stark white. No windows.
John swaggered in late – around 10:30 – everyday,
tugging his pants up in back.
 "Ola." he said. Now why "ola?" John is Greek.
And, every day
he sat down facing out from his desk.
As he landed the chair would creak
while his belly poured over his belt and onto his lap.
Was this the day the chair would break under his weight?
Would John's butt land on the floor?
I took a deep breath, waited, and watched. It never did.

"I'm going to kill someone," he'd say. "Just get me a gun."
Then he'd get up and write down the guy's name on our white board
the killing candidate list we kept hidden behind the cabinet door.
He sat down again, the chair creaked again, I held my breath again,
and he turned. and settled in at his computer to start his day.
But he wasn't quiet for long.
Pretty soon the muttering would start, the foot tapping would start,
And then the cursing.

Now, John is not an Adonis. So don't get the idea that he is some kind of Greek God.

Far from it. He has a huge stomach, he doesn't shave, and his curly salt and pepper

hair is mostly uncombed. He couldn't look handsome if he tried.

He only wears polo-style shirts that he usually drops food on and then he tries to get rid

of the spots with water – leaving more spots.

He kind of swaggers when he walks, trying to suck his enormous belly up and in.

He can't stand or sit still. He paces.

He taps his foot in a rat-a-tat motion that never stops,

The Secret Is Out

Invasive sounds roar constantly between my ears
sometimes sounding like ocean waves,
calm or static hums, or the high-pitched whistle
of an approaching train.
These sounds overshadow
and divert music and voices meant to be heard.
I've lost touch with the sound of silence
Silence is over, caput. It's a dirty shame.

This malady, called tinnitus,
is the first sign of my hearing problem.
There, I've said it. I admit
I'm hard of hearing.

 I ask Google, why hard?
The answer: in early days, it described
all kinds of difficulties: It's hard to learn,
hard to sleep, hard to conceive
I also Google for guidance on cures.

Some say try: Ginkgo bebola,
Lipo flavonoid, special ear-ringing drops
though more of that oily goop flows
out of my ears than remains.
Some advocate therapy cranial-sacral
or neck and head massage.
Others say: keep my mouth open permanently
just like a lipstick model.
Utter humming sounds

from the back of my tongue
and express long, deep, rolling sighs.

Are they kidding? I can only imagine
how the sounds I make on purpose will interfere
with the ones that live inside my head
without my permission.

The truth is the whole list is a bunch of hooey.
Nothing works. There's no known cure.
I have to learn to live with it and not to go stone deaf
as my husband fears.

TRAVELS

Getting Ready

Even while I was on the elliptical
reading about Clark Rockefeller
who had the Rockefeller name
but was not really a Rockefeller,
in my New Yorker,
I kept thinking
should I add a couple of more shirts?
Should I pick out some silver jewelry?
Do I need a pair of dressy high heels?
Even while Jeffery my Pilates trainer
told me my form this morning was excellent
I kept visualizing the piles on the sofa:
shirts, pants, undies, jackets
and other warm wraps,
shoes scattered on the floor,
and the stuff bought
especially for this trip
deep into Kenya and Tanzania –
insect repellent, bite itch eraser,
and a new camera
with a built-in telescopic lens.
Questions gave no respite,
I couldn't focus,
I couldn't stop
wondering what I could add
or even take away?
Even while I was doing my final stretches
that will have to last almost a month,
I knew I still had more to do:

gather my personal toiletries from the kitchen
and bathroom counters
and put them in travel containers,
get out my contact lens solutions,
lay out my clothes to travel in tomorrow.
At least I finished distributing
my vitamins into separate baggies,
at least I had picked everything up at the cleaner
and finished the last load of laundry.
So, no I didn't have to think about
those things anymore.
Yet still weighing on my mind was
how much everything weighs.
Will we get through boarding
onto those small planes in Africa
with only the allowed weight –
a measly thirty-three pounds?

Unstoppable Force

The plane's roar
explodes in my ears.
I can't stop it
turn it off. It upsets
it turns my mind
to mush.
 I must shut down
this unstoppable force
and let it
meld and flow
and mingle with the other
sounds of the day:
the laughing girls
the attendant's requests
the crying up front
the shrieking voice
of the girl across the aisle
until it all becomes
just the noise of the day
and leaves me alone.

St. Paul's Cathedral

This is a religious poem.
Not about my religion
but the religion of St. Paul's Cathedral
in London.
It is large, ornate, but not so
different from other churches
I've seen around the world.
Lots of gold leaf, venetian stained-glass windows,
statuary sculpted out of marble and granite,
and spectacular windows created
from millions of tiny pieces
of glass.
Now we don't get chastised if we don't believe,
but I don't want to be subjected
to that kind of subjugation.
I want religious freedom.
Sure the cathedral is beautiful.
Lots of important marriages
happened there.
but I've got no truck for people
telling me what to do and believe
just as I'm passing through
to see the wonders and artifacts.
No I didn't come there to convert.
I didn't ask for a drowning baptismal ceremony
in the font.

Stonehenge

We drive through farm country.
The fields neatly trimmed
have turned yellow
and dry and hot. Huge rolls of hay lay
every few feet waiting to be picked up
while sheep graze in the sunlight.

We trudge on past
and by the time we stop
we see what we came for.
On barren grass
five-ton stone pillars stand
at attention,
built as early as 300 BC
while other stones
just as huge
lay beaten down on the ground.
They say some bits have already been pilfered
to use as material for other structures
in the ancient past.

Once used as a calendar
to monitor the summer and winter solstice
once thought to protect our civilization.
Now, as we pass
guards must protect them.
We cannot get too near
or touch the stone surfaces

so that generations to come will have
their chance to view
this marvel that no one knows who
built or how.

Vermeers – My Favorites

The Vermeers at the National Gallery
are bountiful. Four from its
permanent collection are there.
One other is on long term loan.
I had never seen any of them,
each of a young woman playing
a lyre or virginal,
one coquettishly looking
toward her teacher standing at her side.
Today the exhibit was all about the music
I could almost hear sounds
like harpsichord pings
as Vermeer's ubiquitous light shone on the faces
of his young girls.
The only thing to spoil the mood
was the woman who pushed
her way up front
and blocked my view.
I challenged her.
She said we allow it.
Well, really! I didn't think the Brits
allow themselves to be
so rude.

Boni

A young person greets us at the airport
in a dress in orange and red
and hair in long tight braids
flowing down his back.
So many beads in primary colors adorn his head,
neck, wrists, and fingers,
at first I think he is a girl.
It turned out he would be our driver
to the lodge and for several game drives
In Kenya's Samburu district.
Besides driving
Boni is a tracker. He looks for footprints
on the bumpy red dirt roads
and fresh dung to indicate which animal
last visited.
Every once in a while
he takes out his monocular
to check in and under the trees,
and relies on his shortwave radio
for sighting news.
When other lodge drivers
spot an elephant family
at least twenty other drivers race
their Safari clients over to gawk.

King of the Jungle

You could fool me
that this animal is
king of the jungle.
He sleeps on his side like a baby
all snuggled up
and peaceful on a warm rock,
his front paws crossed
and mouth gently closed.
Only today, he has one eye
open just a crack
to keep tabs on the
hordes of wildebeest
grazing on the plain below.

Rhino Sightings

Our guides communicate
via short wave radio.
Did you see the leopard sleeping on the rock
and the vultures devouring the dead gnu?
I just saw a male lion over by the big rock
that looks like a man's face.
If you want to get the big points,
take your camp clients over there.
Yet our guide doesn't need many
of those hints.
He seems to know where to go.
He knows exactly where the animals we want to see
hang out.
Yesterday we said we wanted to see a rhino
and he produced an adult walking along
the Serengeti with a child in tow.
Later we said please take us to a cheetah
and there they were – a mom and her two cubs.
Just like he produced the elephants and giraffes.
He just has a knack for it.
Could it be just a hoax
like they say about the moon landing
that guides in this jungle know exactly where to look
and stage our tour as if it's not for real?
No I can't believe it.
Nathan would never do that
Besides he was just as surprised
to see the rhino as we were.

Lions in the Tree

We found them in a little dell
high up on the tree -
four docile lions
too relaxed to pay us any heed.
They looked so calm lying there,
like they didn't have
a care in the world.
Or had they just come back
from a kill,
exhausted from tearing
their prey apart,
eating their fill, and leaving
the rest to the vultures.
No wonder they look so content.
They've done their day's work,
and all that is left
is a big long nap.

Migration

Zebra and wildebeest
march toward the Mara River.
It's time to cross
from one side to the other
as they do every six months
in their quest for more water.
They come in droves.
hundreds of them in long straight lines.
And as they get to water's edge
they stop, look.
A few take the chance
and swim to the other side,
outracing the waiting crocodiles.
The others discuss
in shriek-y honks about when
and at which point to go.
Even though they don't speak
the same language
heads nod in agreement
as they walk en masse in one direction
then to the other,
deciding which is the safest spot
to outwit the croc awaiting its prey.
A few zebras,
the nominal leaders,
step toward water's edge.
They turn, they walk back and forth,
back and forth, and the others follow.
They return to starting point one.
to wait out the crocs again.

I'm Satisfied

On this last day of Safari.
I've seen more animals and birds
than I ever dreamed of –many more
than Noah could ever board in his ark.
The geography varied
in each place we visited
from bumpy hills
with bare trees in Samburu,
a vast plain with little vegetation
called the Savannah in the Masai Mara,
rolling greens covered with dense rocks
and thunderstorms every evening on the Serengeti,
dust and hot dry air in Lake Manyara.
And now at our last place Ngorongoro
wind blows red dusty soil covering
all of me inside and out.

Monet's Lily Pond

Just a few lone blossoms
left upon the pads.
They seem to float
as they flaunt
their crimson and pink petals,
proudly pointing them skyward.
But then an occasional yellow bud
catches the sun's rays
just right.
And we see its
reflection in the pool.

Cote d'Azur

We're swaddled in elegance
here on the Azur coast
where everything is just so.
Huge bouquets of fresh flowers
heavy curtains drawn back and held by fabric rosettes
crisp, freshly ironed tablecloths
(I saw the Maitre D iron them himself)
and forks and knives placed upon them to perfection
While outside the buildings
need washing and the
streets need sweeping.
I'd rather be here inside
in this rarified atmosphere
than out among them
stepping around the
piles left by errant dogs.

Castle for One Night

This morning I was awakened by
singling birds and a whistling wind
so strong it blew the shutters closed.
I snuggled closer to Bob.
And, as he slept, his body jerked beside me.
He was very cold.
Later we walked out in the damp air
knowing by the gray sky the rain would follow
but, not yet.
We had time to explore the paths above
the decaying ruins and statuary
and look down on the aqua swimming pool
and clay tennis court next to
our castle for one night
as if we could lord over all within our gaze.
But, no.
The gray deer got there first.

Many Beds

Tomorrow by this time
I'll be home in my own bed.
That's where I want to be
the most.
Not that our many beds
these last few weeks
have not been wonderful.
Just think about it:
Falmouth just across the bay
from Martha's Vineyard
Boston in a lovely suite with Ben in the
living room,
our first hotel in Paris – funky and seedy
but still friendly,
Toulouse on the capital square in
the Grand Hotel de l'Opera,
then on to St. Remy en Provence – a lovely Hostelerie
just outside of town complete
with swimming pool, golf course and fitness room.
Another move to four days at St. Jean Cap Ferrat
at the elegant Le Voile D'Or where we
ate breakfast each morning looking at the Mediterranean Sea.
Rochegude was next
a 12th Century castle
where I felt like I could master the world, but
only for a few short minutes
 After a drive in the pounding rain
we reached beautiful Annecy and
 L'Auberge de Pere Bise – sometimes haughty

always accommodating
And the most beautiful place of all
next to last – the lovely Lyon Vieux
Lyon's old town and La tour Rose.
I felt so fortunate to be there.
And finally here, back in Paris
on the Left Bank near St. Germaine des Pres
the Lutetia – you can keep it.
It only makes me long for my own bed
all the more.

The End of the Trip

We're both tired
We're both cranky
We're both snappish
Too much driving
Too much packing
Too much unpacking
Too much money spent on food and drinks
That we could easily do without
And too much worrying about mom
And what we'll find at home.
Besides
All of Paris will be closed
On Tuesday
Our last day
No Musee D/Orsay
No Giverney
No Versailles
No shopping
So, forget about them.
Let them rest in peace
They'll have to do without us
We're leaving early
We've already arranged it
And, I can't wait.

The Power of Chocolate

The scent of molten chocolate
wafts through my nostrils.
It permeates my pores.
The small hairs on the back of my neck
stand on end.
I wobble
drunk from the liquor.
It takes over me like thieves.
I warble like geese at a fishpond desiring more.
I would do anything for more –
write an ode to the color, texture, dimension,
the smooth silky feel of it on my tongue,
in my throat, filling my body
weakening my knees,
stopping my heart.

I would bid my lover farewell
and tell him, get down on your knees,
grovel in the dirt before me.
I would tell him, travel the land
and bring me back all the tastes of chocolate.
Go to every city, every town
and find their best samples.
And, I would tell him, go now, at noon
this first day of winter
and come back before the summer solstice
or be gone from me forever.

From Pokerville to Plymouth

Back in the California Gold Rush days
there had to be a place
where those hard-working miners
went to blow off steam.
And Pokerville was it.
Saloons abounded
and pretty girls waited
all gussied up to entertain.
Then the gold rush died.
Yet the town lived on
complete with its hordes of girls
who, all of a sudden
wanted some respect.
They didn't want to be known as
those Pokerville girls anymore.
They campaigned hard,
they marched along Main Street
until the city managers had no choice
but to do away with its infamous moniker.
Instead of Pokerville
the town was henceforth called
Plymouth – a name well-known
for purity – in fact
the epitome of purity.
They couldn't have found a more
pure name in the book.
My only question is:
Where is the rock?

IMAGININGS

He and I

He is Protestant.
I am Jewish. A combination my parents taught me was made in hell
while I was growing up.
No nice Jewish girl would ever consider going out with
let alone marry a shegitz.
I showed them.

He is charming.
I am much too blunt to be charming.
But, I'll take my patience over his charm any day.
He would rather drive through a maze of side streets
than wait for a traffic light.
Every chance he has he'll speed
as I cringe, squeeze my eyes shut, and grit my teeth.
But, I don't say anything.
He ignores my protests of whiplash anyway.

He is tall, once blond, now gray,
with a ruddy complexion and clear blue eyes.
I was short and dark,
now shorter with hair more silver than brown.
He doesn't look a lot different from when I first met him
over forty years ago
except his face has a few lines,
his stomach has grown an inch or two
and he no longer has a crew cut.

He is unbelievably smart.
He still studies, and he would,

if he got the chance,
spend the rest of his days teaching others.
His forte is science and mathematics.
Once he taught a freshman physics class for no pay
just for the love of it.

I don't speak physics. In fact, I'm innumerate.
I got a degree in English,
have a knack for languages
and like to do anything artistic.

Yet my smarty engineer can recite a Shakespearean sonnet at
will.
He won poetry writing awards while in college.
I can't even recite my own poetry by memory.

But, he can't spell.
He always asks me for spelling help
or to finish his daily crossword puzzle.
I know how to spell. I have to know.
I've worked for years turning scientific and engineering
technical gobbledygook and creative spelling
into readable prose.
He is not alone. JFK couldn't spell either.

He spends hours in front of the computer playing games.
I'd rather watch television.
He reads nonfiction and scientific journals.
I like fiction, memoirs and poetry.
And although we both enjoy going to art galleries and museums,
the bar and café easily distract him.
I could look at art all day.

He hates musical theater.
I can remember the words to show tunes
I learned when I was a kid.
But, he'll go if I beg and plead.
He even takes me to the opera.
It's the perfect dark place for him
to tuck his chin into his chest
and take a long afternoon nap.

The Man in the Blue Jacket

A little overdressed
for Manhattan Beach
he walked toward a table by the door,
sat his hulking body down,
and furtively began to punch
into his smart phone.
He looked hot in his dark blue jacket
and slacks, as if he had been
running up hill.
He was not the normal tourist.
His was some other dark business.
A waiter stopped to take his order
"Coffee, black," he said. "That's all."
"But why here," I said,
as I turned to my companion.
"This is not a place for just coffee."
"Perhaps he's here to meet someone,"
my tablemate said,
always ready to give the next guy
the benefit of the doubt.
I looked toward the man again.
He was taking long loud slurps,
wiping up his chin after each.
He really was kind of uncouth,
definitely a dark character who didn't belong
on the patio of this place
on such a beautiful day at the beach.

The Girl with her Feet in the Tub

What should have been a relaxing time
looked like agony.
She never let go
of her pursed lips,
her cringing chin and cheek bones
as her feet were scrubbed,
her legs massaged,
her nails buffed and polished.
She lay back once or twice
showing off her lovely curves
poured into a skin-tight tee.
But even with her eyes closed
her lips didn't stop their pucker.
About forty, she has a
beautiful face,
long flowing dark hair
a figure to die for.
Within the next ten years
I predict those wrinkles
she is cultivating now
will be permanently etched
on her face.

Ashes

How do I write to you, my boy?
You're reduced to a bag of ashes
laid to rest at the base of a tree,
where only an occasional fluttering leaf
can touch you?
You can't hear the bell's tinkle
gently swaying above your grave.
You can't enjoy treats of nuts and figs
sprinkled down by passing birds.

Even the Buddha you fabricated
from a clump of red clay long ago
that guards you as you rest
comforts no more.
You sat like him
with your supple ankles resting
on your knees,
your back against your bed,
so calm, pensive, wise,
concentrating for hours.
Even this meditation
could not save you.
If I had huge amounts
of rubies and diamonds and gold
I could not undo the undoable
and bring you back to me.

So now all that is left are questions:
How could you make such a muck

of our lives and leave us with so much anger?
Why did you guzzle that glass of temptation?
Perhaps it was just too easy.
You let that damn knife do its particular business.
With one swipe you were gone
while the bell tinkles on.

Morning Chill

I woke early,
to a morning chill.
The clock said 5 am,
almost first light.
I moved the thermostat
to bring in some warmth
to our summer vacation condo.
Before I poured
my cup of coffee,
before I went for my morning walk.
I looked in on the boys.

One was missing.
His socks lay by the side of the bed
but he was nowhere in sight.
I began to panic
How often I've gone there
these days.
I went in and out
the screen door
but I couldn't see anyone
to render any help at all.

Then I found a note
that he must have deposited
on the hall table
sometime during the night.
I'm in the closet, he wrote
You guys were making too much noise

up in the loft
I couldn't sleep.

Why me, Lord? I said under my breath.
Why me?

What For?

I walk this morning
ever faster and faster
along the Big Sur coast.
I wear my sweats and my iPod
and listen to Romanza
as the bluejays play in the trees.
The fog hovers over the ocean.
Everything is gray and damp.
My hair gets wet.
Still, I push on.
I don't stop to smell the fresh pine air
I don't stop to hear the waves lapping on the rocks
I don't look for whales in the sea below the cliffs
I'm compelled to push on.
And I ask
What for?

At home
I'm up before dawn every day to get to the gym
I work long hours and weekends
to meet proposal deadlines
I drive myself to write and
I feel guilty if I don't.
And I ask
What for?
Isn't it enough already?
At my age haven't I earned the right to take it easy?
"I'm going to let my hair go
white and cover my expanding body in a muumuu,"

my cousin says.
Hmm, I think. Could I do that?
Probably not.

My mother was 68 years old
when my father died,
I saw her white head in the window
as she sat in her corner of the sofa
after the funeral reception.
And, she sat there for the next 27 years
waiting to die
That's all she could think about
That's all she cared about
And as she waited more of her shriveled away
every day.
Instead I think of Paul Simon's words
"A good day ain't got no rain,
" A bad day is when you lie in bed
" and think about what might have been."
And I keep walking.

Paul

Everywhere I go
Every place I visit
I think of him
My dead son
He is with me
Night and day
In my dreams
More vivid then ever
As if he were wanting
To experience these places
With me or through me
But he cannot
My son, Paul,
Died too soon
He never had a chance
To see the beauty of the world
Or know of such wonders
That could have saved him.
So, I cry for him
My beloved Paul
And all he has missed.

Chicago Days

My grandpa would hoist me high onto his shop counter
caked and shiny with the glues and polishes
he used to cobble and repair shoes.
Once he let me try out his pipe
and I decided to leave it alone after that.
My dad got too big for that scene and we moved north
near Lake Michigan.
Our home had a huge living room
where I dreamed of marrying
in front of the fireplace.
But, too soon we moved again
further north into the suburbs
thick with foliage
that turned bright oranges and reds in the fall.
I rode my bike to school
played team sports,
lost my baby fat,
and fell in love for the first time.
That guy, with a face like Adonis
and a line I bought too cheap,
gave me my first cigarette.
I kicked the smoking habit early, he didn't.
And now he's with Persephone permanently
underground.

About My Name

Madeline – derived from Magdalene – Mary Magdalene, the
wife of Jesus.
Why would any Jewish girl be named that?
Why would any little girl have a name as big as Madeline?
I was the only one. And I hated it.
I wanted a little name.
I wanted a nickname,
But not Maddy.
or Mad or Madeldiny, or Mal or Madalena
No, those nicknames weren't for me.

So, I took ownership of my name
I practiced pronouncing it — Madeline, not Madeleene, not Mad
Ellen
I made sure people spelled it correctly — Madeline, not Madalyn,
not Madeleine
until finally, I grew into it.
Just yesterday, I met someone who said,
"Your name is coming back."
What did she mean?
coming back from where?
It's always been out there.
as far back as Mary Magdalene
It's about time others discover how perfect it really is.

Counterpunch

He said last night was weird
And it was
We couldn't speak to each other
without an upset
so much so that he used
those repulsive words,
that I'm just like my mother,
and left the room.
And he, I thought,
just makes things up.
I didn't holler
I didn't have a fit
I only calmly made a
counterpunch to his complaints.
So even after forty-one years
It is still possible
to go to bed without a goodnight kiss
or even the words goodnight
And I was left to wonder
where I would spend the next night
and the next.

Eighteen

The day she turned eighteen was warm,
it smelled like lilacs
and fresh rose blooms.
Sitting on the garden swing
that hung on the big oak branch,
she kicked her legs back and forth.
She was bored,
her brow wrinkling at the thought
of nothing to do.

Her mother brought the card out to her
thick cream paper edged in gold leaf,
an invitation to attend
her friend Kathy's coming out,
a gold ball at the new ritzy hotel
near the wharf west of the city.
What would I wear to a thing like that?
She continued to kick,
fretting, unable to imagine herself
in any kind of gown, let alone
one in gold.

She sat there for a while,
humming "Wish Upon A Star" softly to herself.
Then she stopped the swing
and ran indoors.
Why not? She'd make the dress.
A long slim skirt shimmering in gold beads
with a sheer halter top.

And her new gold birthday ring
would match perfectly.

Grabbing a cold coke from the fridge,
opening it with a quick flick
at the opener on the wall
she sat down
at the white Formica kitchen table
and began to draw.

Ode to a Racket

Heaven knows
it's just a racket
one used every day
to hit that little yellow ball over the net.
What's so great about it?
Why would a metal frame with gut strings
 mean so much
that one would want to write
a proper ode about it?
Hey, I can imagine accolades
for the nine iron.
At least it gets
the white ball right into the cup
or a horse with such a gallop
earns enough
to fill up a briefcase
with enough money to buy
drinks at the neighborhood pub.
One can forgive a racket
if it fails its master
But odify it, nah
that's just not going to happen.
I know there's no point to it.
Come on, start the engine
Charlie,
lets' get going.
We have to cast the first spell,
over all those
racket masters.

It's time for them to lay low,
stop this nonsense
There's no way in hell
a puny little racket
deserves deifying
with an ode.
Throw them a bone
if they don't behave.

Seventy-Nine

How did I get to be this old?
Just yesterday I was forty
The day before only twenty-five.
I lived all those years
One day at a time
But looking back
They've flashed by like seconds

I don't look seventy-nine
My size two body is svelte
I can still wear spiked heels and
mini-skirts and skin-tight
tees that show off
Perky nipples
And firm breasts

I don't act seventy-nine
I can keep up with the best of them
At the gym or the jogging path
I startle when someone calls me
Madam or automatically gives me
A senior discount
At the checkout stand.

Don't they know
I'm still a young girl
Living inside
An almost eighty woman's skin?

Farewell

You're right
You could say I'm over you.
I'm walking on,
counting the seconds down
until I can
cast you out from
my universe

I feel as suffocated
as an invalid at St. John's
You transport an array of red roses
Every Sunday through Saturday –
That's right.
Every damn day.
You leave tempting bits of chocolate
on my pillow night after night.

You've left me so frayed
I need a laser beam
to smooth out the edges
Find another sucker, buddy
put up your antennas
and I'm sure someone will come along.

And, if no one does
fan the flames of desire
Shine your light down
on some other needy being.
I'm launching on.

The Man on the Cliff

On the cliff overlooking the ocean this morning
his old van, painted white,
was parked a few yards away.
He wore a blue shirt and pants.
One pants leg was folded up
to reach his mid-thigh
where his left leg was cut off.
As we whizzed by I wondered
if this man enjoyed the beauty of the sea,
the clear sky, and the warmth
of this February day.
Or was he contemplating
something much more grave
because such perfection
was more than he could bear.

Even A Broken Foot

Accidents are just that
accidents
Yet some can be avoided
like my husband's the other night.
He walked willy-nilly toward a dark room
that the hotel should have had well lit.
And while groping in the dark
for a light switch
he fell down a short flight of stairs
and was rewarded with immediate pain
in his foot and ankle.
Perhaps a quick application of ice
gave us false hope that it would take
no further care but
elevation, an Ace bandage, and ice.
But more swelling, more pain
indicated x-rays were in order.
The prognosis, a broken foot
not to be walked upon for four to six weeks
Now enclosed in a cast
and crutches prescribed for mobility
there's whining and demands already.
So I wonder
where it says in the marriage vows
for better or worse
and a broken foot?

Four Head Shots

Four head shots in black and white,
the first, a three-quarter view, shows bright,
smiling eyes and a mouth turned up
at the corners with just a hint of a grin.
His hair, so black, it fades
into the background at the top.
A black t-shirt rounds out the effect.

The second is full faced. His hair falls
over the sides of his forehead
and is long enough to peek out
behind his ears. Here he is smiling,
though still with a closed mouth.
Full, dark brows frame deep, friendly eyes
reflect the light of day.

The third, also face on, is more foreboding.
No smile here, he looks serious
like he means business, or he's got a gun.
His eyes are dark, deep set
and tell the truth. So believe it.
He's got you covered.

The fourth is a happy face –
no dark contrasts here.
Just a full, wide smile showing teeth, dimples,
smile lines, and little crow's feet
around the eyes. His jaw is long,
square, honest. This is a guy
you can trust to be your friend
for life.

Reaching for a Star

It used to be comforting to see her there
at her computer as I passed by her office door.
Sometimes we would only nod or say a quick hello.
Other times I would sit in her guest chair
against the wall and we would chat.
I don't remember about what –
maybe our work, her art projects, my poems,
or an exhibit one of us had recently seen
at the Getty, LACMA, or a gallery at Bergamot Station.
Now her door is closed.
Her name is still on it – Adele Yates
with her title – Proposal Process Manager,
but, she doesn't work in there anymore.
Now, we sometimes chat in her nice
third floor room in a tall, white building
on Prospect Avenue in Redondo Beach
where she has her favorite books
and photos, writing papers, art supplies –
even a big screen TV –
all the comforts of home.
Not at a computer anymore,
she sits propped up
in bed in an aqua gown
wearing an oxygen tube in her nose
and a permanent IV shunt in her arm
to receive the doses of morphine that increase
day by day.
As we enjoy her ocean view, she tells me
her plans for her death.

Her ashes will fertilize several gardens
around the world, and her spirit,
happy not to witness anymore catastrophes
of the living world,
will soar to her own personal star.
If all goes according to schedule,
she'll be there in time for her 52nd birthday
in August.

The Moon in the Dark of the Morning

It was a great ball, almost full,
glowing like crystal,
cut into prisms and points,
emanating shooting flames
from all sides
to radiate the misty purple sky.
But soon it engaged
with the rising sun's angry arsenal:
fiery rifle flares
orange and yellow gaseous streaks,
hot red fingernails,
scratching the cold earth
in a hurry to ignite the day.
Still hovering over us,
the stubborn moon
leaves its reflection,
in the liquorish blue water,
like a rainbow of colors,
shimmering within the rippling waves
that bask in the falling moon's touch
until the last moment.

I Won't Know Him

Even though I know him
I won't know him.
I hear he's shrunk in size
down 20 pounds
from his usual husky physique
in just a few weeks.
I hear his speech is fuzzy,
like he's high on drugs,
but perhaps that's a good thing.
He was jovial and upbeat
when I saw him last,
contemplating knee surgery
and spending the last years of his life
in Florida with his grandkids.
Instead, his years of smoking
sometimes four or five packs a day
left his body rampant with cancer.
When I see him next
he'll be in a hospital bed
placed conveniently in his living room
in Queens, New York.
The taut white sheets
light cream coverlet
and stack of extra-thick pillows
support and comfort his every move.
Alongside his bedpost
hangs the morphine drip
that he can tweak ever so slightly himself
to ease his pain.

When I see him tomorrow
this man whom I've known for 40 years
will be a stranger to me.
If only I had seen him two months ago.

Jodi

Jodi works at Timber's
just outside of Green Lake, Wisconsin,
businesslike, efficient, and quick to bring
whatever we ask for.
She takes our orders
with her raspy smoker's voice
and shows great concern
for our dietary constraints.
Is cooking in oil okay
for someone who can't eat dairy,
she wants to know.
I guess those Wisconsin folks
don't understand the difference between
milk from a cow and oil from a tree.
I only wish she'd take better care of her own needs.
She doesn't yet show the deep wrinkles
most smokers wear
or has the hacking cough
that could cause her, her job.
But, that voice is the first clue
that all doesn't bode well
for the rest of her life.

Marnie

She's a little woman
with a big voice
She never stops talking.
but most of the time
I think she's having us on.
She claims to have a man friend,
yet she travels with her lifelong
school girl chum
and then laughs about her man
back home babysitting the dog.
She wears her hair like a teenager
blond, short with bangs cut
across her forehead.
Does she still think she's
in school at the nunnery
waiting for her teachers
to give her permission to grow up.

What I Miss

All I want to do today is wallow in grief,
turn off the television,
shut down all my tech gadgets,
not answer the phone,
keep the door closed and locked,
and ignore my husband's
get over it already admonitions.
I want to think about all
the things he's missed:
9/11, our first black president,
smart phones and Apple's genius bar
that his computer geekness
would have loved.
I want to remember
his jazz improvisations
at his New York and LA gigs,
and how he'd play piano
here in our family room,
his head bent down low to the keys,
his legs crossed imitating
Bach, Jarret, Joplin, Lennon,
and his favorite Miles Davis.
All I ask is to have this one day
out of all the years
I've spent writing, working,
volunteering, and
doing all the diversions
that helped me get by,
just to picture his intense blue eyes

rimmed in lush dark lashes,
his blonde buzz-cut,
his torn jeans and brown leather
book bag slung across his body
as he sat in front of Starbucks
sipping his morning coffee,
and to hear his deep voice calling out hello
as he walked down the long hall the night he died.
After that I'll go back to accepting
that he is really dead,
that he won't be coming back
no matter how much magical thinking I do.
Until then, I want him back in my life today
with undivided attention,
sitting with me here, quietly,
and soothing my heart.
Suddenly I turn to kiss his pale, cool cheek.
And of course, there's no one there.

The Good Wife

What could he have meant when he said,
"I've had a good wife of 45 years."
Could it be that she waits on him hand and foot,
cooks him tasty and nourishing meals,
and never says no when he asks to make love?
Or is this guy who sat next to me
in the front row of the sex education class
required during our senior year in high school
saying it could have been better with me?
Nah. Get out!
That couldn't be it. I can't imagine him
feeling that way about me
after all these 52 years.
We only had a few dates then
and never got past holding hands in the movies
and a peck at the door.
I just wonder why he brought it up
and why he would describe her that way.
The good wife sounds like
he's married to someone
who came over on the Mayflower
and not someone I'd ever want to meet.

Too Tired

What has come over me?
I keep shutting my eyes
tucking my chin in
and then, just like that
I'm asleep.
It's the same at night
I never have a problem
sleeping anymore.
Even if I must get up,
for my nightly bathroom visits
I fall back asleep right away.

This is a new behavior for me
I don't know it.
I don't know what to do with it.
I used to go night after night
without much rest at all.
Now sleep overtakes me.
It won't let me alone.
Is it because of my age?
Will I sleep more now that I'm nearing 80?
Will I eventually want to sleep so much
that it will be all I have left?

Old Married Folks

He walks around the house
letting his privates hang out
beneath the tails of his shirt.
She stands in front of the refrigerator
soup spoon in hand dipping into
the peanut butter jar.
He sits for hours picking out
the right obscure word
to fit into his daily crossword
while she's at the computer
tapping, musing, composing
her daily poetics.

These are the comfortable
married folks. Not yet old
but getting there.
They have learned after
all these years of marital bliss
to give each other space to live
their own separate ways.

A Poem of Farewell

Like the gray cloud eclipsed by the sun
Like a star shooting across the sky
Like the sun's last burst of orange on the horizon
Like the young hummingbird fleeing the nest
Like a baby's sweet whimper before sleep
Like the speeding car disappearing over the hill
Like the period at the end of a page
Like the final credit scrolling off the screen
Like the singing of Aud Lang Syne at year's end
And like Jimmy Durante wishing Mrs. Calabash a goodnight,
My friends, I thank you, and bid you farewell